TABLE OF CONTENT

CHAPTER ONE: Introduction

CHAPTER TWO: What is love.

CHAPTER THREE: What is the Point of Love.

CHAPTER FOUR: Do HUMANS need LOVE.

CHAPTER FIVE: Love - How to show it.

Bonus Chapters.

Chapter Six: Sweet names to call your Lover

CHAPTER ONE

INTRODUCTION

Love is a beautiful thing, no wonder the Supreme Being gave us the commandment to Love our neighbor as ourself. He also confirms love is patient, love is kind. It does not envy, it does not boast, it is not proud. It does not dishonor others, it is not self-seeking, it is not easily angered, it keeps no record of wrongs.

When we are loved our heart starts to feel warm, and your bad mood and impatience melt away. You have experienced love resonating from another person, and it has transformed your experience. This is the power of love; it has the ability to transform an ordinary moment into something magical.

According to scientific research, when we fall in love, our bodies release feel-good hormones and neurochemicals that set off certain, gratifying reactions.

When people are in love, their levels of dopamine, adrenaline, and norepinephrine rise.

All the joy we experience when we are in love is caused by these molecules working in unison. Perhaps this is why we talk about the 'chemistry' of love so frequently.

There are several advantages to unconditional love and compassion. Additionally, they aid in shifting our focus from the narrow "I, Me, Myself" obsession to the wider "We, Us, and Ours".

Also, being profoundly loved by someone makes you strong but being deeply loved by someone makes you courageous." We truly come to life when we are in love. The only thing we can never have enough of is love, just as we can never give enough of it. Love and being loved are the only true sources of happiness in this life.

Chapter Two

What is Love?

Love is one of the most popular themes in artwork throughout history, appearing in everything from songs and poems to novels and movies.

We are made aware that Romeo and Juliet, are supposed to be sworn enemies but fall in love. so they kill themselves because they cannot cope with being separated from one another. Love is one powerful emotion a person can have which is more than enough to unite worlds, turn hatred about and mend broken hearts.

Evidence from history, culture, and even evolution reveals that love existed in the past and in many different places of the world. One study of 166 tribes found that 147 of them practiced love.

The fact that everyone experiences love differently and that it can evolve over time contributes significantly to its uniqueness.

'In love', 'like,' or 'love'?

Over the past 50 years, behavioural studies have examined the distinctions between "in love" and simply "liking" someone.

The definition of like is having favorable thoughts and feelings for someone and enjoying their company. We frequently also feel warm and connected to the folks we like. Sometimes we decide to have an emotional closeness with these folks.

The same good feelings and thoughts arise when we adore someone as when we like them. But we also feel a strong sense of connection and concern for that individual.

All of the aforementioned aspects of being "in love" as well as sexual arousal and desire feelings are included. However, studies on how individuals experience love indicate that not all forms of love are the same.

Here are the seven categories of love, as defined by Greek philosophy:

1. **EROS - ROMANTIC, PASSIONATE LOVE (OF THE BODY)**

Eros embodies all of the qualities associated with the television version of love, including lust, passion, and sexual attraction. Unsurprisingly, the Greek god of love and fertility inspired the name of this kind of love.

This passionate, physical love was exceedingly harmful to the ancient Greeks. The human urge to reproduce is strong, as you can certainly understand, and eros is the kind of love that is simple to let go of.

Eros is purely a physical love, thus you might not want to base your relationship on it (on its own, that is). Eros is passionate, erotic, and, you guessed it, ephemeral.

To establish a solid, complete foundation, a relationship based on Eros should also rely on other types of love.

Eros nonetheless continues to stand for the love of sex and romance.

The passionate, romantic love that is gushed over in all of our favorite books and movies represents this physical connection to one another in today's reality.

2. PHELIA- AFFECTIONATE, FRIENDSHIP-BASED LOVE

Philia is a cordial lover. Those soul-to-soul connections specifically. It includes the affection shared between close family members and friends and is defined by loyalty and trust.

Philia embodies all the qualities of a genuine friend: she is supportive, kind, affectionate, and loving. Despite being totally platonic, it is also touching and deep.

Philia is essentially the kind of love when you merely want what is best for the other person.

The ancient Greeks considered Philia to be even more priceless than Eros since it is a form of equitable love that is shared by those who appreciate one another.

A love connection where Philia is born out of Eros is built to last, just as I indicated that a romantic relationship cannot be sustained on Eros alone. This, according to Plato, is the ideal kind of friendship.

3. STORGE - UNIQUE, FAMILY LOVE

Storge is the term for parents' unwavering love for their offspring. It is a kinship-based, protective love that embodies acceptance, sacrifice, and approbation.

Storge resembles philia in appearance, but it is more unilateral. Imagine it as the love a mother has for her child, whether or not the youngster feels the same way.

In essence, it is a solid connection and affection created through necessity and familiarity.

Another way to look at storge is in the affection you have for your sister, even if she was always stealing your favorite clothing when you were a kid.

Right there is pure, unwavering love!

4. AGAPE—SELFLESS, UNIVERSAL LOVE

Agape is a special sort of love. It is a compassionate, genuine love that extends to God, nature, total strangers, and the less fortunate.

Agape has connections to selflessness, which is viewed as an altruistic, sincere concern for the welfare of others, rather than depending on familiarity (as does storge).

Many people believe that agape is a type of spiritual love that manifests through meditation, nature, intuition, and spirituality.

This, according to Christians, is the love that Jesus had for all people. Since the Greeks felt that only few people were able to experience it over the long term, it is sacrificial and highly radical.

Agape can be compared as a kind of love that is rcciprocal in today's society. It is a kind of love that demands nothing in return and merely makes you feel happy.

Agape is not only connected to improved bodily and mental health, but some people also claim it leaves them with a euphoric high.

5. **LUDUS - ACTIVE, FLIRTATIVE LOVE**

Ludus means carefree love. Ludus is acting on his crush by being playful, flirtatious, and uncommitted. It is the infatuated stage that appears in the beginning of a romantic relationship.

If you've ever experienced love, you'll understand what I'm talking about.

"Like in the story of the Strangers where two parties had fun while it lasted. They got to know what they both liked after they explored each other's body intimately.

Receiving a message or a phone call to come over or meet at a certain place, and no one else knows what you are up to. The mystery behind this is mischievous and dangerous, but subconsciously the fact remains your company is only needed at that time to be enjoyed.

They were not clear at the start about what they wanted, and that is why they went wrong. The Strangers wondered if they were clearer at the beginning, would things have been different. In the end, they couldn't see a future with themselves.

They drifted apart and became strangers just like the people we walk past on the street every day".

I picture a brief encounter when I think about Ludus. An unrestricted kind of conquering. Your stomach is filled with those usual butterflies.

Think of flirting, dancing, teasing, seducing, all the jazz—whatever fun means to you—because that's what Ludus is all about.

Relationships that arise from this kind of love are undoubtedly on the casual side, but it doesn't imply they won't last.

Long-lasting Ludus partnerships can produce a light, undemanding, and adorably uncomplicated kind of love as long as both people have the same perspective.

6. PRAGMA - COMMITTED, PERMANENT LOVE

"The passion

I want to start by congratulating my parents on your silver anniversary, managing not to kill each other or my brother, sister and me. I also want to thank all of you for being here today and helping us to celebrate this very special day for our family

I wasn't there when the love story of my Dad and Mum blossomed (I came about 3 years and 9 months later ;)) but on every single account, especially my Mum's, my mum was the typically hard to get Filipino girl

There is one story (that they've told us a few hundred times) when they were dating and had a massive argument, probably started by my mum, who stormed off the bus they were riding and into the crowded streets, leaving my Dad abandoned and lost.

Luckily, my Dad loved my mum enough to look for her and keep loving her.

The love story that I do know is a beautiful love story written by God. A love that as they grow older, the more in love they fall. On this day, 25 years ago, they probably thought they loved each other so fiercely and completely. That love does not compare to the love that they share now and the love they will have 25 years from now.

It makes me smile when I see the way that our Dad looks at our Mum, even though sometimes it makes my siblings and I embarrassed. Especially when they kiss in a photo booth and stick the photo on our fridge where our friends can see when they come over.

When we were much younger, we lived on the second level in an apartment and every day, my mum would know exactly when my Dad got home because she could "smell" him, even 2 stories up. My mum can't even leave the house without kissing my Dad goodbye. My sister reminded me of a time when she and my mum were in the car about to leave to go to work. My Dad came out of the house, looking annoyed and when my sister asked, "What's wrong with Dad?" My mum answered, "I haven't kissed him goodbye yet."

Mum and Dad, thank you for being an awesome example of love. Thank you for setting the bar high, showing us the kind of love that we should strive for and one that we deserve.

Separately, you are two amazing people, but together you are complete.

Please raise your glasses while I toast my Mum and Dad on 25 wonderful years.

Even now, coming up to their 30th anniversary, I see the love of my parents growing. I see how even at their age, they're still growing as individuals, still pushing each other to be better and loving each other more because of it".

Pragma is love that considers the long run, to put it simply. In many long-lasting relationships, such as marriages and friendships, pragma is evident as love.

It is based on dedication, perseverance, friendship, and sharing similar aspirations for the future, such as starting a family and establishing roots.

Many people (married people in particular) will interpret Pragma as "making it work."

This kind of love develops when a couple spends year after year together and is welcoming and durable.

The older married couple who have been together since they were teenagers comes to me when I think about pragma.

They continue to hold hands and look at each other after 50 years of marriage. Who wouldn't want it eventually, really? Pragma is lovely because it symbolizes the ongoing care required for a committed partnership.

It is matured, tolerant, and sacrificing, and in all truthfulness, it is pretty uncommon.

7. PHILAUTIA - LOVE YOURSELF

The ancient Greeks understood philautia, or self-love, as a healthy, necessary love of oneself that enabled one to offer and accept love from others (Haven't we all heard the adage about how you can't pour from a bucket that isn't full?).

The development of self-worth, self-confidence, and the rise in self-esteem required for a feeling of purpose go hand in hand with healthy manifestations of philautia.

We cannot give what we do not have, to paraphrase the Greeks. If we don't love ourselves first, how can we ever love others?

Philautia is thus comparable to self-compassion. It is crucial to love and care for ourselves in the same way that we love and care for others.

There is, of course, an opposite. If we are not careful, philautia can develop into a disease. While the Greeks did not intend for this to happen, excessive self-love can lead to self-obsession and a sense of superiority.

Philautia can develop into narcissistic behavior, arrogance, and selfish inclinations when it becomes problematic.

It's crucial to strike a balance between one's love for oneself and that of others.

Chapter 3

What is the Point of Love?

Although passionate love begins off strong, research on how romantic love changes over time often reveals that it dwindles during the duration of a partnership.

This is due to a number of factors.

Routines evolve as couples get to know one another better and grow more certain about their future together. The likelihood of experiencing novelty and excitement, as well as the frequency of sexual activity, can both drop. This may cause intense affection to fade.

Even though not all couples experience a decline in their passionate love, according to numerous research, 20–40% of couples do. The biggest decline is most likely to occur in the second decade for married couples who have been together for longer than ten years.

Experiencing passion might be difficult due to life's transitions and happenings. People's competing obligations drain their energy and reduce the chances for fostering passion. Parenting is an illustration of this.

Companion love, on the other hand, is usually observed to grow over time.

Although studies show that most romantic relationships have both passionate and companionate love, it is loving and committed love—rather than passionate love—that might have a negative impact on a relationship's ability to last.

People's bonds and commitments to one another are maintained through the emotion of love. According to evolutionary psychology, love developed to keep couples together so that their offspring may live and develop into sexually mature adults.

For humans, childhood lasts a lot longer than it does for other species. Love is especially vital to humans since children depend on adults for many years to survive and to acquire the knowledge and skills necessary for successful life.

It's difficult to imagine how the human species could have developed without love.

Regardless of the variations in how love is felt or described, one thing unites all of us as social animals with a strong interest for it (LOVE).

Chapter 4

What best describes Love?

1. First, "Thinking as 'us,' not'me.'"
2. "When sex turns into true romance and love making."
3. "Taking on the world together."
4. "Holding hands and completeness."
5. "Wiping his eye crust away and tears."
6. When dedication is a privilege
7. "Bubble baths together."
8. Every second I'm aware of his or her presence.
9. "I only wanted to be at home."
10. Eating takeout while wearing pyjamas.
11. Building a project "greater than myself,"
12. Knowing that everything is, in fact, fine.
13. Aching without him here."
14. Squeezing hands during the movie
15. Decisions for us, not for me.
16. Support during highs and lows.
17. "Agreeing that being together is best for us."
18. Best buddies with sex.
19. Saying a lot without using words.
20. "Always choosing to advance.
21. Impulsively grinning, feeling so lucky.

22. when your person is your "home."
23. "The thrill of delight and fantasy."
24. Adoring each and every oddity.
25. "That emotion every time I see him or her."
26. "Silly faces for laughs, bursting with happiness just because."
27. Feeling as though you have conquered life.
28. Without considering "the end," fighting.
29. "Matching tattoos and clothing."
30. "Eyes on each other, not expensive gifts."
31. The greatest need is for them.
32. Holding hands "simply because."
33. Forgiving even when they are in error
34. "Laughing until someone poop's."
35. "Suddenly, I'm lot less afraid."
36. "Comfort and understanding at the next level."
37. "Experiencing extreme vicarious pain."
38. Alongside them, I was enjoying the silence.
39. Trust with weed-like roots.
40. allowing her to do my fingernails
41. "His calming influence."
42. "Sacrificing their body, soul, and mind in worship.

43. "What drives me to continue."
44. when escaping is not an option.
45. putting her life above mine.
46. Without holding back or feeling guilty, sharing.
47. In someone else, I find myself.
48. beyond anything else, choosing their firm.
49. Truly at ease all the time.
50. "In good health and in bad."
51. "Really, the purpose of life."

So to the question?

What best describes Love:

____

CHAPTER FIVE

Love: How To Show It

As a relationship specialist, I do offer some suggestions as this is not a one-size-fits-all lesson.

One of the most common human emotions is love, although its definition is still complex. Often, you can simply sense it and know. Strong feelings of attachment and affection may be triggered by just a quick glimpse at the individual. Because love is an action as well as a feeling, it's possible that you'll experience an intense desire to make that person happy. To truly love someone, one must provide for them unconditionally in the ways that they require support.

Love: How To Show It.

Be Dedicated to Your Relationship

Make the decision to be in the relationship, to work for its development, and to provide the greatest possible care for it.

Without that dedication, you lack the solid groundwork for creating a meaningful connection. That is why the initial step is so important.

Find out how they desire to be loved.

You and your partner are the only ones who understand what it means to love one another. Every relationship and every person on the earth are special.

Finding out your partner's "love language" is a good place to start. It is a loving act also in itself to talk to your partner about their love languages and then modify your efforts accordingly. These include kind words, gifting, touching gestures, spending time together, and doing good deeds.

Quality Time:

Your complete attention is the only way to show someone you care about them.

You put down your phone, turn off your tablet, and pay attention to your partner when you're with them. And when you do that, you make a genuine emotional connection with them. It gives people the impression that you intentionally set aside time for them, making them feel special, appreciated, and valued.

Quality time with our relationships is sadly getting more and more difficult to come by because of technology. We are always somewhere else, usually in cyberspace or lost in our own thoughts, even while we are together.

No matter how long you sit there, being near to someone while doing something else is not necessarily considered meaningful time. And this lack of connection might make your partner feel lonely and empty if their major love language is quality time.

In a situation where couples stay apart each other as a result of border, job or other circumstances. Continuous, persistent, conscious communication is key also sustained efforts must be made to manage the issues which distance breeds like loneliness, non-frequent sex, lack of emotional and physical support.

Couples should be open to each other and honestly express challenges they face. They should help each other and try to overcome challenges together.

Give them some room.

Codependence is love without limits. Setting limits entails recognizing where one person ends and the other begins, and time and location play a significant role in this division. Giving your partner the opportunity to put their own needs and wants first is necessary for a good relationship, even if it means letting them spend some time alone concentrating on their own life—their career, health, friendships, or artistic endeavors. In a relationship, neither party should feel perpetually in charge of the other's happiness, especially if it comes at the expense of their own. Remind your partner to take care of themselves and assure them that you will always be there to support them.

Practice being accountable.

Love entails accepting accountability for one's own actions. Acknowledging your errors, apologizing, and recognizing your partner's point of view are all challenging since they call for vulnerability and humility. Show your partner that you are not afraid of a little discomfort if it means standing up for what is right.

Accountability is reciprocal as well. Holding your partner accountable for their mistakes is necessary if you love them. No one benefits from keeping things inside out of concern for offending someone's feelings.

When arguing, use restraint.

While it's crucial to resolve disputes as they come up, love should always be present as you work through them. There are respectful methods to argue, such as avoiding finger-pointing and emphasizing "I" comments. Additionally, refrain from using generalizations like "You never" or "You always."

Additionally, it's critical to avoid being defensive, aggressive, or closing down. Instead, resolve disagreements amicably, with humor, interest, and transparency, and be careful to respect your partner's viewpoint.

Surprise them.

Surprises have the ability to impact your regular routine and provide your partner a special memory.

The fact that it's unexpected is crucial since it demonstrates your independence by demonstrating that you made the decision to prepare it yourself.

These can include sending flowers to her at work, cooking her a delicious dinner if she usually does the cooking, going on a picnic, writing him an old school love letter, buying him something he has been eyeing, or making plans for a weekend getaway.

Gift.

Gifts are a heartfelt, non-materialistic approach to show your partner you care because they provide as a "visible reminder of the love that you carry for them,

Giving gifts is a fundamental component of all relationships. You undoubtedly have no shortage of reasons to give your beloved a gift, but do you know why they are so important?

Giving your sweetheart a gift does not imply that you are trying to purchase their affection. You are also not required to give things to express your love. Consider presents as an addition. Even a tiny present occasionally has the power to express feelings that you are unable to. Gifts can also demonstrate your affection for your partner and your attention to his or her wishes and requirements.

Simple take on this: Gift suffice when words cannot.

"Thank you"

One way to express love is surprisingly simple: Just tell them. "It sounds so simple, and yet we don't do this enough,

Research has shown that being grateful has numerous psychological and physical advantages, and this holds true for romantic relationships as well.

An example "I appreciate how you consistently go above and beyond to show me that you care. I never imagined that I would come across someone as kind and considerate as you. I appreciate your love and kindness."

Give your loved one a sincere thank you, even for seemingly insignificant things.

Interest and Listening

Always express interest in your partners world, a simple how was your day goes very far to soothen his or her mood if actually he or she had a rough and tough day . Also when you show interest always listen. Listening is very key because this expresses interest.

Concluding Remarks

The most beautiful thing there is is love. The most magnificent present you can offer is your love. Genuine actions of love cannot be substituted by heartfelt sentiments or butterflies in the stomach.

It need much more than that. It requires a commitment, an action, and a decision that are repeated over time.

Everything you need is right here. It's the beginning you require to see your connection through to completion. Apply the aforementioned advice for a week or a month. Watch to see what eventuates.

\

Chapter Six

Sweet names to call that special lover

When you are dating someone, there comes a point where addressing him or her by name sounds strange.

Right now, calling your partner by name sounds awkward; instead, give him or her a nice nickname or moniker.

You will also need a cute contact name for your lover at this point of the relationship so that when you are called, this cute nickname will show up on your screen.

But it's not always simple to come up with a cute nicknames . Don't worry you can pick from here or better still use this to form that sweet name.

What cute nicknames can you give your lover?

Give a moniker that reflects your lovers appearance

Give a moniker that reflects his or her character

Come up with funny nicknames by changing his name.

Give a moniker based on his or her profession.

Based on your lover characteristics and peculiarities, give a moniker.

Give a moniker based on his or her position.

Based on his or her characteristics and peculiarities, give a moniker.

Using interests and favorite items as a guide, give a nickname.

Give a moniker based on how much he or she resembles a well-known person.

Use cute names from TV shows, video games, songs he or she likes or from my "BOOK".

The names listed below are sweet nicknames you can use for your HE.

Ace – An excellent nickname for a boyfriend who is a genius.

Acushla – An Irish term that means "pulse" or "vein."

Adonis – A very handsome boyfriend.

Zeus – A boyfriend that is powerful.

Zorro – A good nickname for a boyfriend that defends you always.

Baby Boo – A cute name for a boyfriend you like a lot.

Baby Boy – For a guy who is very dear to you.

Cakes – A sweet and adorable guy.

Candy – A fantastic name for a boyfriend who is so handsome and sweet.

Captain – A cute nickname for a reliable and handsome boyfriend.

Yum Yum – A nickname for a happy guy, who always looks great.

Yummers – A boyfriend who's too kind and sweet-natured.

Captain America – A boyfriend that always saves the day.

Dare Devil – A guy who does an impossible stunt.

Daring – A boyfriend who is adventurous and brave.

Sweet Heart – For the sweetest boyfriend ever.

Sweet Honey Boo – A term of endearment for a guy who spoils you silly.

Sweet Kitten – A kind-hearted and gentle boyfriend.

Sweet Lips – A boyfriend with really enchanting lips.

Darling – A boyfriend you love dearly, and really appreciate.

Baby Bugaboo – A nickname for a boyfriend who gets jealous easily.

Viking – A guy that will tear down walls for you.

Violet – A boyfriend with an exhilarating personality.

Vita Mia – For a guy who's your life.

Volcano – An intense boyfriend

Baby Butter Fingers –A fun nickname for a clumsy guy.

Enigma – A cute name for a weird and mysterious guy.

Ever Guy – A great name for the guy you want to be with all the time.

Everything – A boyfriend who is extremely important to you, he means the world to you.

Baby Cakes – A pet name for the love of your life.

Adopted Bro – A guy that could almost be mistaken for your brother because of the bond you share.

Xoxo – A nickname representing hugs and kisses.

Adopted Twin – A good nickname for a guy who's your best friend. You do everything and go everywhere together.

Popeye – A great nickname for a vicious boyfriend.

My Superman – A boyfriend who has great strength than other men.

The names listed below are sweet nicknames you can use for your SHE.

My vibe - Someone who gives comfort, joy and happiness when you around her.

All Mine – A special girl that is yours.

Amore – For someone that you love.

Bae – For the most amazing person in your life.

Cherry Pie – For the sweetest person, you know.

Firefly – A charming girlfriend who's always all over the place.

First Lady – The most important lady in your life.

Flame – A cute name to call your beautiful girlfriend.

Flash – A very athletic girl with fast legs.

Flawless – A girlfriend perfect for you.

Cherub – A girlfriend that is full of life and great vibes.

Chick – For a young and attractive girl.

Chickadee – A cute pet name for a hilarious and troublesome girlfriend.

Jewel – A sweet name for a very special girlfriend.

Joy – A girlfriend with a giddy and optimistic nature.

Juicy – A lady with a high sex drive and who's always horny.

Ballerina – For a dancer or a girl full of grace and poise.

Lucky Charm – A girlfriend who brings luck to you.

Bam Bam – A cute name for a girlfriend who is full of so much energy.

Bambi – For a beautiful and classy lady.

Heart & Soul – A girlfriend who completes you.

Hot Chocolate – A girlfriend dark, sweet and sexy.

Misty Eyes –A girlfriend with those irresistible puppy eyes

Hot Lips – A girlfriend with attractive and skilled lips.

My Everything – A girlfriend who is irreplaceable.

My Girl – For a girlfriend who's just right.

My Heart – A sweet name for a girlfriend who is indispensable.

Heart Throb – A girlfriend who wholly owns your heart.

Angel – An affectionate name for a girlfriend who has a beautiful heart.

Pancake – A girlfriend who is savory and sweet.

Ride Or Die – A cute nickname for your forever girl.

Sugar – A girlfriend who's sweet, alluring, and enticing.

Rollie Pollie – A girlfriend with a taste for adventure.

太后 (Tai Hou) – It literally means "Queen".

Feel free to add yours.

1.____

____

2.____

____

www.ingramcontent.com/pod-product-compliance
Lightning Source LLC
LaVergne TN
LVHW020534160826
845677LV00015B/4046

* 9 7 9 8 8 4 6 4 9 2 2 9 5 *